VYACHESLAV KOZITSYN

WAR
PHOTOGRAPHER

peko
PUBLISHING

1.1

INTRODUCTION

© PeKo Publishing Kft.

Published by
PeKo Publishing Kft.
8360 Keszthely, Bessenyei György utca 37., Hungary
Email: info@pekobooks.com
www.pekobooks.com

Responsible publisher
Péter Kocsis

Author
Vyacheslav Kozitsyn

Printed in Hungary

Photos
Péter Kocsis

First published
2019

ISBN 978-615-5583-20-9

All rights reserved. No parts of this publication may be reproduced, or transmitted in any form or by any means, electronic or mechanical, including photocopying, recording or by any information storage and retrieval system, without permission from the Publisher in writing.

This new photo book series presents various selections of rare wartime photographs. They will be selected based on numerous subjects. Each volume introduces photographs from battles, operations, vehicles or complete photo albums from soldiers who fought in World War Two.

This book illustrates photos from an unidentified German Sturmartillerist of Sturmgeschütz-Abteilung 191. This unit was dispatched from Jüterbog in December 1940, and the unit moved out southeast on several trains. Its final destination was Romania and the path ran through Czechoslovakia, Austria and Hungary. Sturmgeschütz-Abteilung 191 began its combat path in the Balkans. The album contains photographs from heavy fighting at the Greek border where the Abteilung's assault guns supported the advancing German infantry on the Metaxas Line, photographs taken during marches through the country depicting the destruction and broken enemy vehicles, and a short stay by the Abteilung in Greece after the capitulation. You will find photographs from the entire combat route of Sturmgeschütz-Abteilung 191 in the USSR and several pictures from Romania and Serbia, taken after the evacuation of the unit from the Crimea. Photos from 1941 show broken Soviet tanks, trains and artillery pieces, and German assault guns in the harsh Russian winter during the battle of Moscow. 1942 is shown in the form of several shots during the recuperation of the Abteilung after an unsuccessful offensive on the Soviet capital, a journey of many kilometers to southern Russia. The subsequent 1943 and 1944 years are not as extensively represented in the photographs as the previous years, but among these few photos are shown several Sturmgeschütz III, photographed after the Abteilung's evacuation to Crimea in 1943 and during the battles there.

After arriving at the destination (the center of Romania), parts of the unit distributed to different cities and villages under their own power. Some episodes of these transfers are shown on this page.

St./StuG.Abt.191 was located in Mislea. There are photos taken on the territory of a prison and, possibly, in other places of Mislea. Most of the damage to the buildings on this page are the result of an earthquake.

A column of five R-2 [similar to German Pz.Kpfw.35(t)] of the Romanian army on one of the streets of Bucharest. The Romanian army received a significant amount of these Czech tanks before the outbreak of World War II.

Good view of the beautiful natural landscape in the Romanian mountains, located in the counties of Brasov, Dâmbovița and Prahova. The path of the German army to these mountains lay through the city of Sinaia.

The Sturmgeschütz-Abteilung 191 personnel move south toward their location. Thanks to the tops of the majestic mountains in the background and the surrounding area, we managed to find the exact place where this photo was taken. During the photo shoot, the car with the photographer moved approximately between Poiana Țapului and Cumpătu. To the right of the German cars flows the river Prahova, which did not get in the shot.

StuG.Abt.191 crossed the Romanian-Bulgarian border through the cities of Giurgiu and Ruse in early March 1941. After that, the Abteilung continued to move in a southwesterly direction, towards the Balkan Mountains. These two photos were taken near the town of Veliko Tarnovo.
This page below: The German servicemen wash and shave on a March morning. The motorcycle in the photo is the K500 Zundapp.
Next page: The light car, shown in the bottom photo from the previous page. This is the Stoewer 200 (Luftschutzwagen Kfz.4) with the Zwillingssockel 36 anti-aircraft gun with twin MG 34 machine guns. These cars served as the main standard protector of Abteilung batteries against enemy aircraft.

Two members of StuG.Abt.191 are posing with their vehicle, a Wanderer W23 S. The photo was taken in the same place as the photos on the two previous pages. In addition to the emblem of the unit on the right front mudguard like many other vehicles shown on the previous pages, we can clearly see on its left mudguard the tactical marking showing that this car belongs to StuG.Abt.191.

The main combat power of an assault gun unit, one of its batteries. According to KStN 446, the table of organization for a Sturmbatterie in an Sturmgeschütz-Abteilung adopted in July 1940, the batterie was supposed to include 6 Sturmgeschütz III (3 platoons of 2 vehicles each), 4 Sd.Kfz.253 (one for each platoon and one for the batterie commander) and several other light vehicles. One of the four Sd.Kfz.253s of this batterie is in the foreground of this photo. These lightly armored vehicles were designed to observe the battlefield and coordinate the firepower of assault guns. Judging by the markings on the hatch in the rear plate of this half-track observation vehicle, this is 3./StuG.Abt.191. The self-propelled guns in StuG.Abt.191 had a letter identification system. Only two of the six Stugs seen here have their white letters visible on the engine starter hatch covers. The closest Stug has the letter "F", while the vehicle in the distance with only one spare wheel on the roof of the engine compartment has the letter "C". Perhaps all six of these Sturmgeschützs are arranged in alphabetical order.

The column of cars continues to move along the road up the mountain slopes. The column includes the Wanderer W23 S and Mercedes-Benz 170 VK Kfz.2 cars from St./StuG.Abt.191 and several other light vehicles.

This page: Residents of one of the cities in the Balkan Mountains took to the streets to meet a German column. The Sturmgeschütz III Ausf.B from this page shows bent metal rectangular plates in front of the indicator lights on both track guards. This is another distinguishing feature of assault guns from this unit, in addition to letter identification, large 'Balkenkruez' and spare tracks under the exhaust silencers and on the rear part of the fenders, shown on page 13.
Next page: The solemn greeting of the German military continues. The 20-ton armoured fighting vehicle and several trucks almost completely dissolved in this huge crowd of German soldiers, officers and locals of all ages. In the center of events are several young Bulgarians who arranged dances and German officers in the first row of spectators.

Members of St./StuG.Abt.191 during the halt between marches on the way to Sofia. The Abteilung reached this city in the second half of March. The car with the number 'WH 199 713' looks much cleaner than the car in the center and the motorcycle, although they all traveled the same many kilometers along dusty plains and winding mountain roads.

The unit left Sofia at the end of March 1941. It moved south and, reaching the town of Dupnica, it continued along the Djerman river. The next destination was the river Struma. The Abteilung moved along this river to the border with Greece. This photograph was taken during a halt somewhere in the valley of the Struma river in early April 1941. Two lines of trucks are surrounded by several other cars, motorcycles, Sd.Kfz.252 and 253 and one StuG III Ausf.B. The servicemen are engaged in various activities: some inspect and maintain the equipment, others bring water, while others simply lead the conversation or lie down to rest on the grassy hill.

This photo, also taken in the valley of the Struma river in early April, shows us a great view of the whole Sturmgeschütz Batterie. The main combat power in the form of 3 platoons of assault guns (2 vehicles in each platoon) is lined up on the right. According to K.St.N. 446, each platoon inside the Sturmgeschütz batterie must be accompanied by one Sd.Kfz.252 and one Sd.Kfz.253. We can see one of these lightly armoured vehicles near each StuG platoon, some Sd.Kfz.252 have additional trailers. A fourth Sd.Kfz.253, parked amongst three light cars, is probably the command vehicle for the battery.

Above left: Latest photos from friendly Bulgaria.
Right: Crossing the Bulgarian-Greek border in the Kulata region, April 6, 1941
Below left: Tombstones of servicemen who died on the first day of Operation Marita (Germany's invasion of Greece). One of the tombstones has the name of a soldier from schwere Artillerie-Abteilung 616, which was part of XVIII. Gebirgskorps with Sturmgeschütz-Abteilung 191.

German units received several days to recuperate after the long battles on the Metaxas line. This page shows two photos taken during the march after this break. Here vehicles from Sturmgeschütz-Abteilung 191 pass a destroyed railway bridge across the Struma River, April 12, 1941.

Several photos taken in different places of central Greece during the marches of the unit in mid-April 1941.

A knocked out British Vickers Light Mk.VIB Tank with traces of burning on the rear of the turret and an abandoned Universal Mk.I Carrier can be seen. In the foreground on the post is a sign to indicate the location of the 2.Panzer-Division.

StuG.Abt.191 received an order to move towards Thessaloniki at the end of April. These photos of Luftschutzwagen Kfz.4 and the German motorcyclist against the background of the destroyed bridge were made somewhere on the way to Thessaloniki. The exact location and date of the photographs is not known.

Despite the rapid advance of the German troops in central Greece and their superiority over the enemy, they could not avoid casualties. Shown here are the graves of unknown German soldiers, photographed on the way to Thessaloniki or in the area of this city.

Forming up on the shores of Thermaikos Bay northeast of Peraia at the end of April 1941.

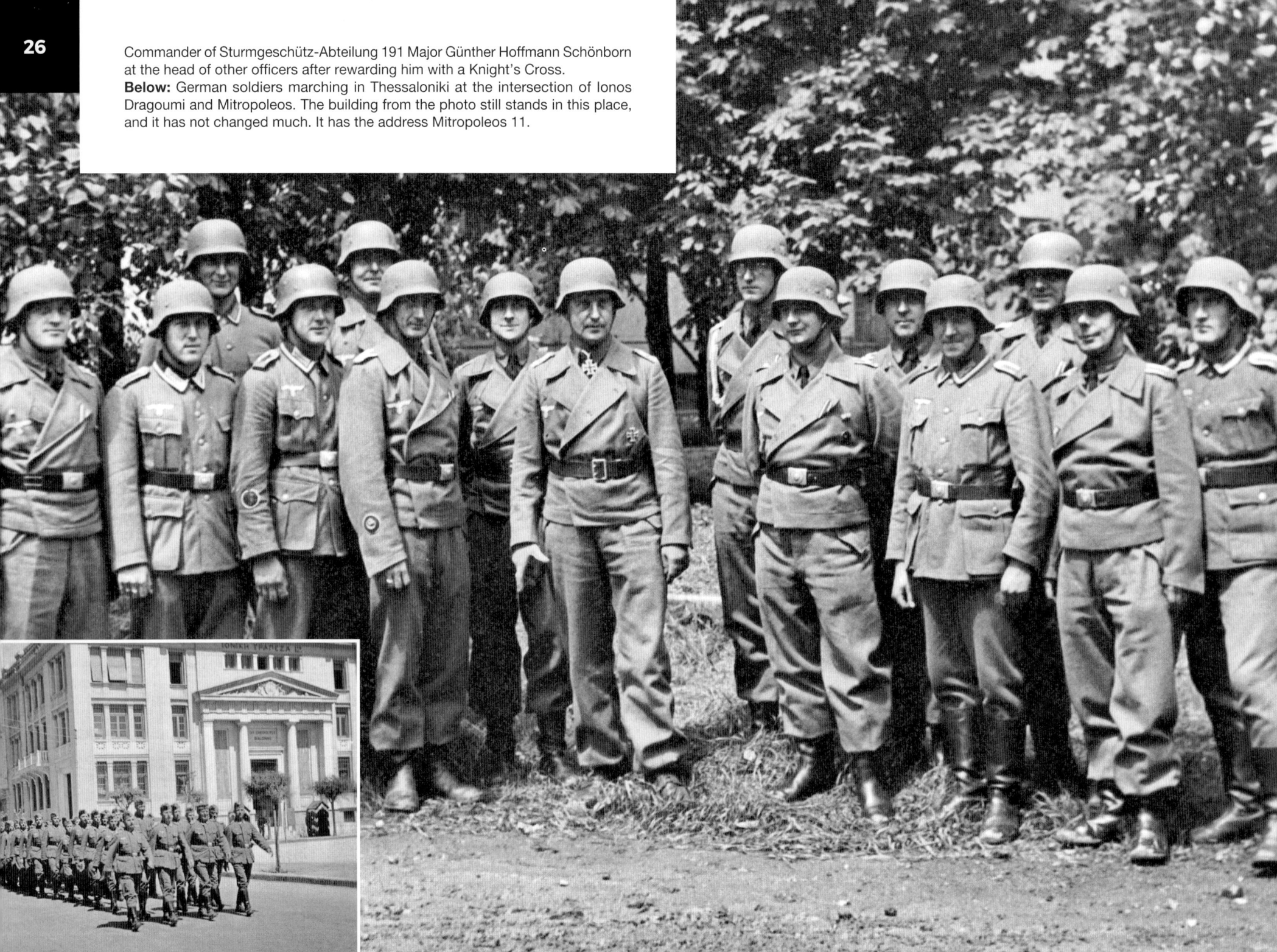

Commander of Sturmgeschütz-Abteilung 191 Major Günther Hoffmann Schönborn at the head of other officers after rewarding him with a Knight's Cross.
Below: German soldiers marching in Thessaloniki at the intersection of Ionos Dragoumi and Mitropoleos. The building from the photo still stands in this place, and it has not changed much. It has the address Mitropoleos 11.

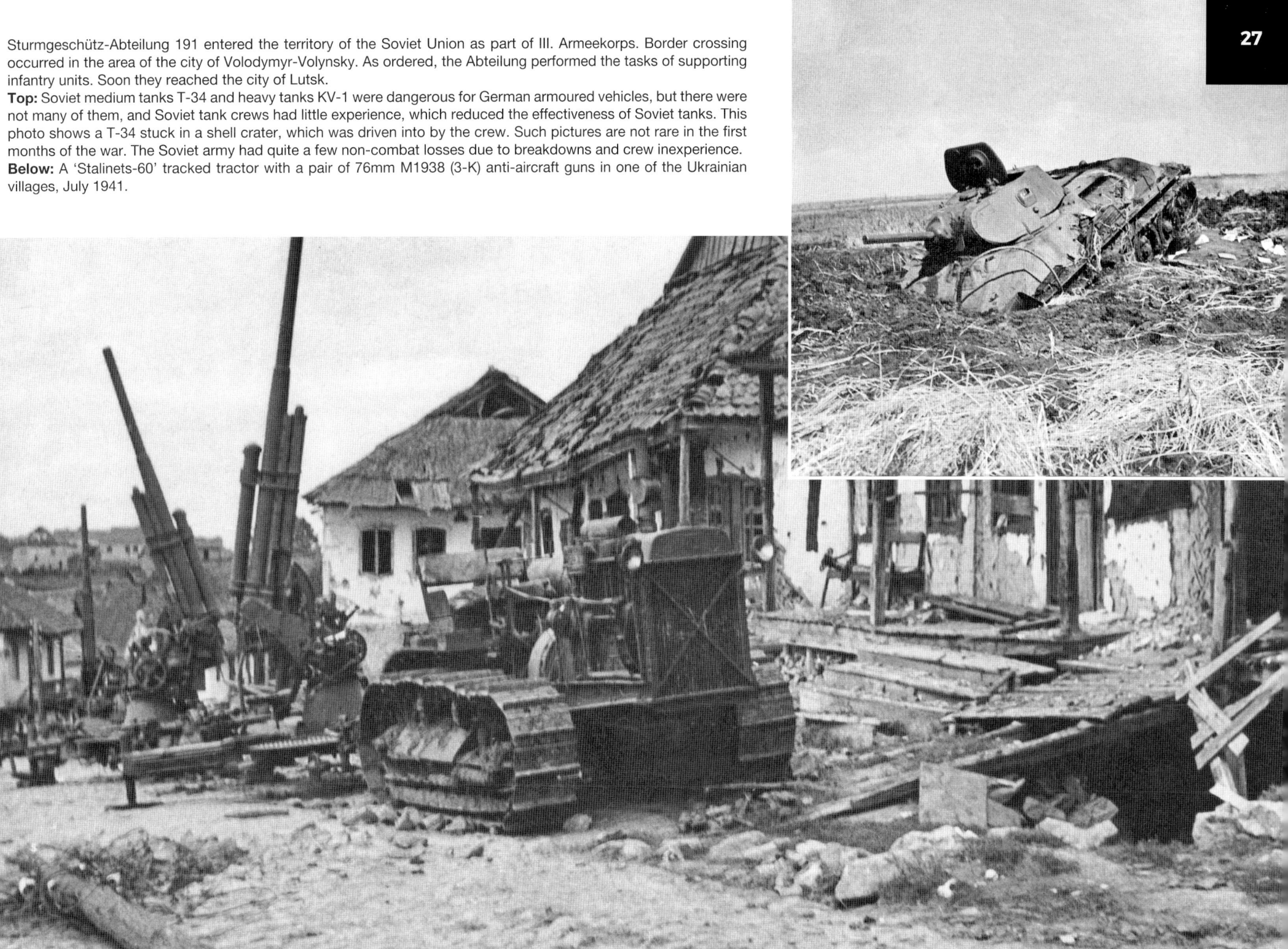

Sturmgeschütz-Abteilung 191 entered the territory of the Soviet Union as part of III. Armeekorps. Border crossing occurred in the area of the city of Volodymyr-Volynsky. As ordered, the Abteilung performed the tasks of supporting infantry units. Soon they reached the city of Lutsk.

Top: Soviet medium tanks T-34 and heavy tanks KV-1 were dangerous for German armoured vehicles, but there were not many of them, and Soviet tank crews had little experience, which reduced the effectiveness of Soviet tanks. This photo shows a T-34 stuck in a shell crater, which was driven into by the crew. Such pictures are not rare in the first months of the war. The Soviet army had quite a few non-combat losses due to breakdowns and crew inexperience.

Below: A 'Stalinets-60' tracked tractor with a pair of 76mm M1938 (3-K) anti-aircraft guns in one of the Ukrainian villages, July 1941.

The branches with vegetation for masking this Sturmgeschütz III Ausf.B could be very useful, since the armor of the self-propelled guns was powerless against the Soviet 45-mm armour-piercing shells, and the Soviet 76-mm tank guns could pierce even the front armour of the StuG III from medium distances. Despite the camouflage vegetation on this StuG's armour, we can still see several signs of StuG.Abt.191, such as the protective metal plates in front of the light indicators on the track guards, spare tracks on the back of the track guards and the unit insignia behind the gun cleaning rod.

Another disguised StuG III Ausf.B. The relaxing infantrymen in the foreground could be personnel from 44., 298. or 299. Infanterie-Division. The photo was taken in the Ukraine during June or July 1941.

A destroyed train with one T-34, a pair of T-60 light tanks, ammunition and other equipment. There are numerous unexploded shells and various bits of wreckage in front of the railway cars.

Right: The defeated column of light Soviet armoured vehicles, which include T-26 light tanks and a BA-10 armoured car. The burnt out T-26 in the foreground has penetrations from German projectiles on both sides. This column could have been destroyed by the tanks of 13. or 14.Panzer-Division.

Bottom: One of the real giants of the Soviet tank forces, the KV-2 heavy tank. These tanks, with their impressive 152mm howitzer and rather thick armour, were valuable trophies for the German servicemen.

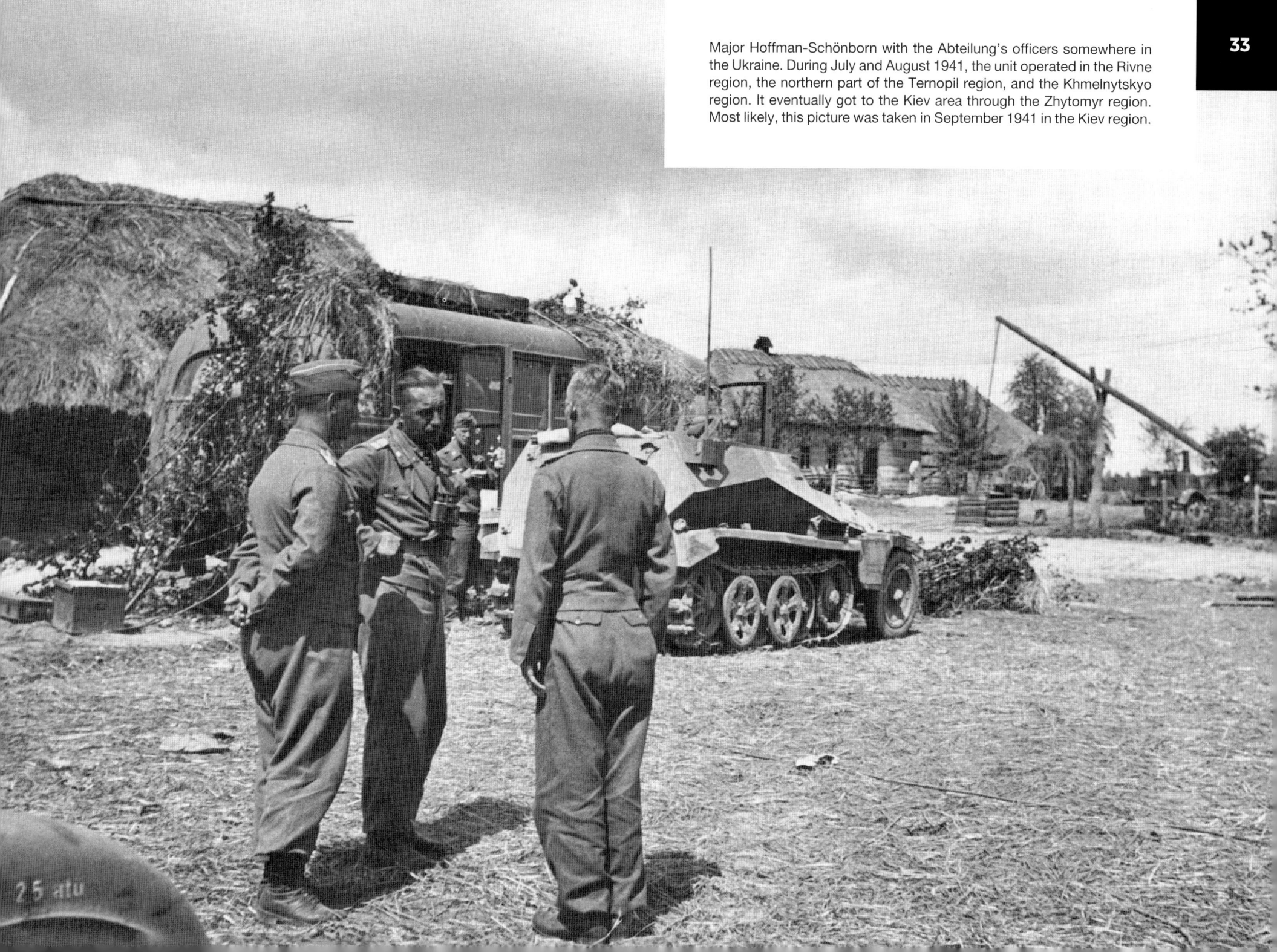

Major Hoffman-Schönborn with the Abteilung's officers somewhere in the Ukraine. During July and August 1941, the unit operated in the Rivne region, the northern part of the Ternopil region, and the Khmelnytskyo region. It eventually got to the Kiev area through the Zhytomyr region. Most likely, this picture was taken in September 1941 in the Kiev region.

An Sd.Kfz.253 and a Matford F917 WS, stuck on a muddy stretch of dirt road somewhere in the Kiev area, the end of August – September 1941. The French truck has the emblem of 113. Infanterie-Division on its door and the soiled nose of the German armoured observation vehicle has the insignia of Sturmgeschütz-Abteilung 191. Both the 113th and 191st, together with other German units, crossed the Dnieper River north of Kiev at about the same place and later they could be found together in the fields of the Kiev region.

Another episode of overcoming the Soviet dirt roads. This photograph, taken at the end of the summer or in the early autumn of 1941 somewhere in the Ukraine, shows a group of several 'Borgward' B3000 from StuG.Abt.191. The towing vehicle did not enter the shot, but we can make the assumption that its power was not enough to pull the trucks out of the mud and now the servicemen are waiting for the arrival of a more powerful vehicle for help.

The process of replenishment of ammunition of assault gun between the battles. This Sturmgeschütz III Ausf.B has several traces of splinters on its frontal armour and a lot of light damage, such as deformation of the track guards and the destruction of the main headlights and their cover. Pay attention to the detail above the hole for the gunner's sight in the frontal armour of the superstructure. This is a mount for the machine gun, located in front of the commander's hatch. Crews of assault guns were forced to resort to similar non-standard solutions to protect against enemy infantry at close range until the moment when all the StuGs began to be equipped with standard machine-gun shields in front of the loader's hatch.

This page: StuG.Abt.191 arrived in the Belarusian city of Slawharad and then in the area of the city of Roslavl in the first half of October 1941 to support the German troops advancing on Moscow. The Abteilung participated in heavy battles and almost all the time was moving forward to the capital of the USSR. In November 1941, the unit reached the Moscow Region, where photographs were taken from this page. This page shows the new Sturmgeschütz III Ausf.E, which began to be produced in October 1941. This one entered into the inventory of StuG.Abt.191 quite recently, and it is not painted in winter white camouflage, but already received the emblems of the unit on the right mudguard and on the side armour of the superstructure near a 'Balkenkreuz'.

Infantrymen and crewmembers assess the damage to another Ausf.E from StuG.Abt.191. This vehicle has additional road wheels, fixed with metal strips in front of the superstructure armour. The track's rupture, damage to some of the road wheels, and light damage to the track guard are caused by the assault gun driving on a mine.

Sturmgeschütz-Abteilung 191 left the Moscow region after the breakdown of the German offensive on Moscow and some time later was located in the neighboring Kaluga region. Later, the Abteilung went to the rear area (Belarus) to recuperate. On this page members of the support service and their trucks are on the outskirts of Mogilev, spring 1942.

The forming of personnel of Sturmgeschütz-Abteilung 191 in their temporary residence on the outskirts of Mogilev. The unit commander participates in the presentation of awards. The bottom right photo on the next page shows three winners, one of whom is the commander of 1. batterie, Heinrich Kollböck (standing to the right). In the future, he will become the commander of the Abteilung.

Having received new Sturmgeschütz III Ausf.F with long-barreled guns and after restoring the winter losses, the Abteilung was ready to take part in the hostilities again. The unit left Mogilev in early June and it was already in Kursk in the middle of the month.
Above: officers discuss the route of the Abteilung's vehicles, June 1942.
Below: new assault guns overcome a small river somewhere in central Russia, June 1942. New StuGs received camouflage in the form of long curved stripes over the base dark yellow colour.

A halt during the many kilometers marching through central Russia. The StuGs have additional boards on the upper part of the aft hull armour to hold the stowage on the roof of the engine compartment. Note that the colour of the barrels of the 7.5cm guns in this photo are different from the main colour of the rest of the vehicle.

This page: Three other assault guns from StuG.Abt.191, also having boards at the rear of the engine deck. The tarpaulin covers the front of the superstructure, unlike the vehicles from the previous page, so that we can see what lies on the roof of the engine compartment: spare tracks, a lot of jerry cans and several boxes.

Next page: These pictures were taken at one of the points of a multi-kilometer march. During the summer of 1942, the Abteilung crossed almost half the country starting in the Mogilev region and ending in the north Caucasus. Some of the StuGs from these photos have sandbags on their superstructures; perhaps they were placed there for the convenience of people who want to sit outside the compartment during their long journey. The superstructures of other vehicles are supplied with additional tracks. All assault guns are covered with the same camouflage and have no markings except for the standard 'Balkenkruez'.

A member of Sturmgeschütz-Abteilung 191 and the road markings of the location of his unit. The distance to Berlin is a bit exaggerated here, while the distance to Jerusalem is almost twice the true distance. Four signs with multi-coloured buffalo emblems can mean St./StuG.Abt.191 and the Abteilung's three batteries.

A burial place, where two members of Stabsbatterie/StuG.Abt.191 were buried. Both of them, as well as a few servicemen from another unit, whose graves are in the background, died at the end of August 1942. The photo was taken approximately in the central part of the modern Stavropol Territory in Russia.

A neighborhood of Mozdok, September, 1942. The German servicemen inspect a knocked out Soviet armored train 'Nikolay Schors' from the 19th separate armored train battalion. It was destroyed as a result of the battle with German tanks in August, while the German troops also suffered considerable losses.

A group photograph of StuG.Abt.191's personnel somewhere in the area of Mozdok during the autumn of 1942. After the battles in the area of this city, the Abteilung began to move north-west for subsequent evacuation to the Kerch Peninsula in the Crimea.

Sturmgeschütz-Abteilung 191 left Novorossiysk in mid-September 1943 and it continued to retreat to the north-west via Anapa. The unit took part in heavy defensive battles at the Taman Peninsula in late September. The assault guns supported 50., 98. and 370. Infanterie-Division, as well as some other German units. An evacuation of StuG.Abt.191 into Kerch took place in the first half of October. The photos from these two pages show the moment the Abteilung's personal moved across the Kerch Strait.

StuG.Abt.191 concentrated around the villages of Leninskoye and Novomykolaivka (about 30 km. East of Kerch) after the evacuation to the Crimea. We can see the Abteilung's new assault gun on this and the next page. These photos were most likely taken somewhere near these villages in the middle of October 1943. Judging by the Schürzen and the design of frontal armour of the hull, this StuG III Ausf.G was built in the period from March to May 1943. At first sight, this vehicle looks new, but the Schürzen have multiple traces of operational service, which suggests that this StuG was used at the front for several months. StuG.Abt.191 took part in battles in the area of Krasnoperekopsk (in the north of the Crimea) and in the area of Kerch in November and December 1943.

53

Crimea, spring of 1944. The burnt fuselage of the Soviet I-153 or I-15 aircraft apparently lies in this field since 1941. The aircraft of this model were obsolete at the time of the start of the war, but they were sometimes used in 1941. In addition to this fact, we can see the abundance of vegetation around the aircraft with traces of a strong fire, which confirms the supposition that much time has passed since this aircraft fell.

This 'Tiefladeanhänger für Panzerkampfwagen' (Sd.Ah.116) has damage to one of its wheels. One of the men in the photo adjusts the height of the lifting jack, and the other two are busy replacing the wheel. All 10 lug nuts from the wheel have been removed and they are lying on the platform above. The adjacent tire has a wheel chock to keep the trailer from rolling, and the axle is supported by a complete return roller and mount from a Sturmgeschütz III. The load area of this Sd.Ah.116 is occupied by a knocked out Volkswagen Type 166 and a large number of tracks of different types.

The process of evacuating a destroyed assault gun from 1./StuG.Brig.191 (StuG.Abt.191 was reorganized into Sturmgeschütz-Brigade 191 in February 1944) from the battlefield somewhere in the Crimea, 1944. The towing vehicle is a heavy half-tracked Sd.Kfz.9 tractor. It stands still and wheel chocks are under its tracks to prevent it from rolling down the hill. Based on the way the winch cables are arranged, it appears that this machine is being used as an anchor and a second Sd.Kfz.9 that is not in the photo is being used to pull the Sturmgeschütz.

Disabled Sturmgeschütz III Ausf.G from the previous page. Its running gear has been completely destroyed: roadwheels, return rollers with their mountings are damaged and the idler wheel is torn off. The vehicle's side has at least 4 holes from Soviet projectiles: the first hole is in the superstructure side plate, the second is in the track guard near the front part of the superstructure, the third is behind the broken second return roller and the fourth hole is near the idler wheel mount above the last roadwheel. Pay attention to the last hole as an S-shaped towing hook has been inserted into it. Such an abundance of hits provoked an explosion inside the fighting compartment and a subsequent fire, which destroyed most of the rubber tires on the roadwheels. The features such as single piece transmission hatches, non-standard offset location of the driver's shot deflector and the design of the track guard support brackets indicate that this Sturmgeschütz III Ausf.G was built by MIAG in the fall of 1943 on the chassis of a Pz.Kpfw.III Ausf. L or M.

Russian troops launched a massive offensive in the Crimea in April, 1944. StuG. Brig.191, along with other German and Romanian units, gradually retreated to Sevastopol and the Brigade left Crimea in May. The members of StuG.Brigade 191 are posing in the port town where the Brigade arrived in mid-May 1944.

The return of the Brigade to the front began in the autumn of 1944. The personnel of the unit were again taken to the southern section of the Eastern Front, to the Serbian city of Niš. Heeres-Sturmartillerie-Brigade 191 (new reorganization and name at the end of July) was ready for hostilities in early October. The photos from this page may have been taken in September or early October, when the unit's staff was in Serbia and it was awaiting full completion of reorganization.

COMING SOON